# Drug Detection Dog Training

**By IAN TINNY**

with information provided by Dr. Rex Curry

ISBN: 10:1500735280
ISBN-13:978-1500735289

# DEDICATION

This is dedicated to all victims of drug detection dogs, and to victims of modern prohibition in the U.S.'s police state.

Many mysterious events inspired the author to pursue a ten-year investigation of drug dogs. The trail of evidence precipitated a deep plunge into the shadowy world (of which most lawyers and judges are unaware) of using drug dogs for lies and perjury. Drug detection dogs are used to violate the rights and freedoms of individuals everywhere.

This story reveals untold secrets of drug dogs that weave from the old prohibition, to modern prohibition, and to the present police state and its constant growth, forever changing American history as we know it.

This book is dedicated to all the people who have been, and who will be, persecuted, beaten, jailed, and killed, via the dishonest use of drug dogs. You are modern heroes.

This book is also dedicated to the hapless dogs conscripted into the police state's insanity.

DISCLAIMER: No animals were harmed in the making of this book.

On the other hand, many dogs have been injured (and have died) in the police state's modern prohibition. Many humans have been harmed, too. Many humans have been deceived, threatened, robbed, beaten, arrested, imprisoned, and murdered under modern prohibition and the use of drug dogs.

# CONTENTS

# ACKNOWLEDGMENTS

If you are about to read these revelations for the first time, then I envy you, because of what you have ahead of you. The discoveries exposed herein have changed many people's lives. Perhaps, they will change yours too.

I feel indebted to many good friends for help and advice in the preparation of this book. Many do not want to be named due to fear of repercussions from the police state.

Special thanks are due to everyone who is brave enough to see what others refuse to see, and to speak the truths that others cannot face.

My inspiration for this book came largely from the work of Dr. Rex Curry, an attorney and historian, living in the United States.

It gives me great pleasure to see this book appear in distribution worldwide after being handsomely printed through the effort of a distinguished publishing firm in cooperation with a new literary establishment. This book is long overdue.

# 1

# AVOIDING DRUG DETECTION DOGS

A book exposing drug dogs should begin with the best advice: How to avoid them in the first instance. The way to avoid drug dogs is: Avoid the police.

Drivers should pro-actively prevent cops from following in traffic. Police have ticket and arrest quotas that have led to the planting of drugs, to corruption, and to deaths.

If you are able to see a cop in your rear view mirror (no matter how far back the cop is), then you should turn and either take a different route, or circle the block, or pull into a gas station or convenience store.

If you are on the highway and it is possible to take an exit, then do so. If possible, re-enter the highway after the officer has passed.

If there is a cop at an intersection ahead of you in a position where you will pass and he might end up behind you, preemptively turn before you pass the cop's location. Change your route, or circle the block so that the cop will have proceeded elsewhere, or so that he will be ahead of you.

It should go without saying: Don't ever pass a cop. If a cop appears in front of you, then you should remain a long way back, or take a different route. Don't pass.

If a cop is behind you and then follows you after you turn, then you should immediately find a place to stop (e.g. pull into a gas station, convenience store, or fast food location, then exit your car and go inside).

In other words prevent cops from being in a position to read your tag, and prevent them from being in a position to pull you over. You might save your own life and the lives of those who are with you.

# 2

# EXPOSING THE FRAUD
# OF K-9 SNIFFER DOGS

Drug dogs are used for lies. They are used to fabricate "probable cause" to search cars (and other conveyances, objects, and packages).

Judges write clueless opinions in which they wonder about how accurate drug dogs are, and they overlook this point: Police can lie and say that the dog alerted when the dog did not alert at all. It does not matter how accurate drug dogs are.

The most common excuse for police dogs is modern prohibition: the insane War on Drugs.

The word "police" comes from the word "policy" because police enforce the policies of deranged politicians on the local, state, and federal level.

The word 'politics' is derived from the word 'poly' meaning 'many', and the word 'ticks' meaning 'blood sucking parasites.'

Blood-sucking parasites on dogs compare favorably to blood-sucking parasites who use dogs for lies in order to steal millions of dollars from law-abiding citizens under the police state and its Civil Forfeiture laws.

Cops lie like dogs. Cops lie like rugs. According to grammar rules, the second sentence is ungrammatical because, for rugs, the word should be "lay," and not "lie." And dogs are not dishonest, but they do want to lie on the floor. Cops tell lies about drug dogs, and they use drug dogs to tell lies about humans. Perhaps this tweaks it: Cops lie like a dog on a rug during a July day in Florida. In other words, they lie a bunch.

Drug dogs are natural libertarians with no interest in modern prohibition, and they have to be constantly taught and reinforced (brainwashed) to detect drug odors, and to approach peaceful humans and search them, so that humans can be arrested, handcuffed, and imprisoned for decades. That is not an easy trick to teach a dog. It is easier to teach humans.

Drug dogs are a reminder of similar police-state tactics and obsessive Gestapo behavior under the National Socialist German Workers Party.

Police officers should not be forced to endanger their own lives (and the lives of innocent dogs) enforcing modern prohibition and initiating violence against peaceful people engaged in non-violent consensual conduct.

The following paragraphs describe how narcotics dogs are used as ruses against humans, to violate constitutional rights against searches and seizures -


* NEVER CONSENT TO A SEARCH. Consenting to a search means that the driver is waiving his rights under the Fourth Amendment of the U.S. Constitution. If consent is given, and the police either find or fabricate a reason for an arrest, then any motion to suppress based on an illegal search will be opposed by the prosecution with the truthful argument that the victim/defendant "consented" and waived his rights. If a victim/defendant consents and then tells his lawyer "they had no reason to search my car," part of the lawyer's response will include this: "It does not matter because you consented to the search. You waived your rights. That makes it more difficult for me to help you."


*Cops ask to search cars for no reason at all during routine traffic stops. Cops ask to search because they know that most victims are ignorant about the fact that drivers should "just say 'NO!'" (most drivers are know-nothings about constitutional rights). Drivers who do know are often too frightened or meek to say "NO!"

It is unknown how often cops ask for consent to search. It is unknown how often consent is given under duress or ignorance. Drivers who do not complain roadside will not complain later, and will not learn, and will not litigate later.

The police use of "consent searches" has inspired opponents of the practice to educate the public with the slogan "Say No To Searches!" and "Say No To The Police State."

\* If drivers say "no," then cops tell drivers that a K-9 unit has been requested by police radio, and a sniffer dog is coming to the scene, and that a longer ordeal is therefore inevitable if the driver will not "consent" to a search of the car. That warning is often a lie to induce consent. There is no police dog on the way.

\* Whether or not a dog is in transit, some cops add additional lies to make drivers think that there will be a long wait, and that the driver must stay until a dog arrives. Cops rely on driver ignorance of the fact that evidence will be suppressed if drivers are detained longer than it takes to complete the traffic stop (e.g. write the ticket). Drivers are induced to consent to search to avoid a long wait based on lies. Cops will say things like "You should consent to search, because the dog is going to scratch your car up," which is a threat of property damage made to induce consent, and it is also an indication of a badly trained drug dog (if it is true), and a bad handler.

* Learn to say "AM I UNDER ARREST? OR AM I FREE TO GO?" Some cops let drivers think that they are obliged to stay even when the cop has no reason to detain drivers any longer. Cops rationalize that drivers inexplicably loiter roadside with cops, or that drivers enjoy waiting for dog sniffs. Cops take advantage of drivers who are too stupid (or too meek) to ask if they are free to go, so that drivers "consent" (in the rationalization of cops) to unwarranted detention by not leaving.

* Cops lie about how long it takes to write tickets or to obtain a radio response on a tag inquiry, or license inquiry. If a dog is actually en route, then some cops write tickets very slowly, until the dog arrives.

* Even after the dog arrives at the scene of a traffic ticket

stop, cops still try to obtain "consent to search" because cops think that they can more easily avoid suppression of evidence motions that expose the cop's falsehoods, reveal the dog's inaccuracy, destroy the dog's future credibility, and force the dog to be retired, and necessitate a new dog (puppet) to replace it (until that new dog is exposed). With the dog at the scene, cops will repeat statements such as "You should consent to search, because the dog is going to scratch up your car."

*What happens if a dog is discredited in a court proceeding that reveals the dog to have a high error rate? There appears to be little that prevents police from re-naming the dog, moving it to another location, or taking other actions to continue using the dog for its originally intended purpose: as a ruse to fabricate "probable cause" for searches.

*Another reason why police use drug dogs is the same reason why felons use large menacing dogs: as substitutes for guns, in order to threaten and terrorize people. Video recordings of some drug dogs makes it appear as if they have been trained to bark continuously and to leap and lunge. Some "drug dogs" are also trained to be attack dogs. That can be dangerous if the dog becomes confused about its purpose in a particular situation involving a civilian.

* Police ask for consent because they have no "probable cause" to search. When victims persist in refusing to consent to a search, police take advantage of court cases from judges who opine that police can gain "probable cause" if a properly trained and properly handled drug dog gives a bona fide "alert" indicating that the dog smells the presence of illegal contraband in the car. A search is forced against the driver's will.

*Police fabricate "probable cause for a search" by lying and claiming that a canine alerted, when the dog did not alert. A search is then forced against the driver's will. Video recordings on the web show these police lies, including videos where the dog handler walks the dog to the front of the victim's car (where the dog handler deliberately hides from the police car's dashboard camera), and the dog handler loudly proclaims that the dog is alerting, while there is no view of any alert by the dog on the video.

If drugs are not found hidden at the front of the car (and drugs usually are not found there) then that fact should be used in a motion to suppress evidence because it shows that the dog did not alert, or that the dog's alert was an error. The same argument should be made whenever drugs are not found near the spot where a drug dog allegedly alerted on the car.

*Police manufacture "probable cause for a search" by cuing a drug dog, to induce it to "alert," if the dog is not alerting on its own. Police lie and claim that the dog properly alerted. A search is forced against the driver's will. Victims need to pay close attention to the dog and its handler, make a video recording (and also use any police dash camera recording) to expose the truth.

Cuing can be deliberate or subconscious (dogs may imagine that the handler desires the dog to alert). Sometimes it is not clear whether the cue is deliberate or subconscious. For example, if a dog handler repeatedly walks the dog around a car it could be cuing that is deliberate or subconscious. The handler might know from past experience that if he walks the dog around the car enough, the dog will eventually interpret that as a cue and alert. Motions to suppress evidence should argue that a dog should circle a car once (because if drugs dog are as amazingly accurate as cops claim, then one circle is enough). Any additional circling is cuing (because the cop is angry that the dog did not alert on the first walk).

* Many errors by drug dogs cause lawyers to wonder if police carry drugs to plant scents so that drug dogs will alert. Some news items support such speculation in cases where drugs have been planted by police. Drug prohibition is wrong, and its wrongfulness is

compounded by government during enforcement of "modern prohibition."

* If a narco dog alerts and nothing is found in the resulting search, then cops will never record that as an error by the dog. If confronted by the apparent error under cross-examination, cops will testify (testi-lie) that the dog detected lingering odors of contraband that were recently present. Cops will testify that dogs never make mistakes, never have and never will, and that apparent errors are, in reality, the dog's skillful detection of residual odors of contraband.

No one can question a dog about whether the cop is lying or mistaken, and it is usually a waste of time to ask a cop the same types of questions.

Police like dogs because the dogs cannot be cross-examined. Defendants are denied their constitutional right to confront witnesses against them.

A motion to suppress should be filed because experts will testify that drug dogs can be trained (and should be trained) to ignore residual odors. Dogs that are not trained to ignore residual odors should be considered incompetent to provide probable cause for a search.

* Motions to suppress in court should argue that the drug

dogs cannot provide probable cause because "drugs are everywhere." Drugs are on the ground (in restaurants, bars, streets) and can transfer to shoes when people step on the wrong spot. Drugs are then transferred to cars from shoes. Drugs can be on the ground underneath the spot where a car is stopped by police. Drugs are on roads and in parking lots and can transfer to the tires and underbelly of passing cars (this is an explanation of why a dog would alert on parts of a car where no drugs are found). Drugs are in the air, blown by the wind, to land on passing cars. Drugs can be in the rain that falls on cars and dries, leaving a residue. Drugs can be on the hands and clothing of police from earlier arrests. Drugs are on paper money and then transferred to the hands, pockets and clothing of innocent people who handle the money later.

* Drug dog fraud is about more than cops stealing drugs. It is also about cops stealing cars, money and other valuables. Under the police state's civil forfeiture laws, police will lie and claim that large sums of money are "drug money." Police will steal the money, even if no drugs were found and no arrest was made. Police will bolster their lies that the money is drug money with additional lies that a dog alerted on the car (even if no drugs were found). Police use civil forfeiture laws to steal cars, money, real estate, and other valuables. Under civil forfeiture laws, police can engage in theft without

finding drugs, without filing any criminal charges, and without convicting anyone of a crime. Regardless of any criminal charges, the theft of the victim's property becomes a separate nightmare.

# 3

# DRUG DETECTION DOG TRAINING

Drug dogs are similar to humans in that dogs must be taught to approach peaceful people and search them, so that humans can be arrested, handcuffed, robbed, kidnapped, and imprisoned for decades under modern prohibition. That is not an easy trick to teach a dog. It is easier to teach humans.

Sniffer dog skills are often overestimated because people anthropomorphize dogs.

A dog's skills should be under-estimated because the most humanlike quality that dogs have is that they are natural libertarians with no interest in the war on drugs.

Drug dogs are trained by playing a game. The dogs

are taught using toys. The toys are hidden with drugs to trick the dog into a game of searching for its toy by associating the toy with drug odors.

A drug dog's training is not unique or complicated. Many canine house pets will search for a toy that is hidden under a sofa pillow or a coffee can. The toy can be hidden with a package of cinnamon or some other item with a unique odor. After a few weeks, the cinnamon can be hidden alone, without the toy, and the dog will find the cinnamon via its smell, a smell that the dog was taught to associate with its toy.

Many errors can happen due to the training method. There is always the danger that a drug dog will alert on anything that resembles or smells like its toy (towels, tennis balls, car carpet, etc.).

Errors occur if a dog smells anything it desires or wants to attack or investigate: if a cat was carried in the car; if another dog has ridden in the car; if there is the odor of food in the car.

A Reuters news report stated that a San Diego arena was evacuated for about two hours, delaying a first-round game in the hugely popular national college basketball championship, after a hot dog cart attracted the attention of a bomb-sniffing dog. Thousands of fans arriving for a game between Marquette University and the University of Alabama were kept outside. Authorities cordoned off part of the building. It was meat, and not explosive heat, attracting the dog's attention.

Many drug dogs are so inaccurate that they could be replaced with the "drug coin." Flip the "drug coin" and if it lands on "heads," then that means that there is an alert and that there is probable cause to search. If it lands on "tails," then that means there is no alert, and that there is no probable cause (but a search occurs anyway).

Drugs dogs often bark up the wrong tree. In the U.S. Supreme Court case of *Illinois v. Cabelles*, Justices Souter and Ginsburg dissented, pointing to studies showing that drug dogs frequently return false positives (12.5 to 60% of the time, according to one study).

Sniffer dogs are trained to detect only specific contraband (e.g. cocaine and marijuana). Some dogs are trained to detect only a single drug (e.g. only marijuana). To attack a K-9, determine what drug(s) it was trained to detect. If an arrest was made based on an alert for a substance that the dog was not trained to detect, then that should be part of a motion to suppress arguing that the alert was an error, or that it was a lie. One example would be: if a dog trained to detect only marijuana allegedly alerts and a search reveals only cocaine, then an arrest will occur for the cocaine despite the apparent error by the dog. Police will not volunteer any information about the fact that the dog was only trained to detect marijuana.

If an arrest is made based on a search by a drug dog,

then a motion to suppress the evidence should be filed based on the arguments in this book including any evidence of cuing, the behavior of the dog at the scene, inadequate training of the dog, inadequate maintenance of the dog's training, a history of false positives (or a lack of record keeping regarding the dog's false positive rate) and various other problems that might be evident based on the timing and conditions during the detention of the victim and the search.

If a search occurs via the use of a drug dog, and no arrest occurs, then the police should be sued civilly based on the arguments in this book.

Under the current statist quo [sic], if contraband is found then the arrest will probably stand. If nothing is found, the driver leaves shaken, but there are few cases where the driver complains or sues. Bad police are emboldened by the fact that people will not take action after bad searches.

It doesn't matter whether a drug dog is accurate. The dog is present at the scene as a cover-up so that when the officer is called to testify he will "testalie" in court. Dogs are perfect pets for perjury.

Any case that lacks a videotape of a dog's actions on the scene should result in  rejection of testimony that the dog alerted, or that the dog alerted without cueing.

Drug dogs differ from humans in that the natural

libertarianism of drug-dogs always resurfaces, and must be suppressed constantly by law enforcement retraining. Without constant reinforcement, the dogs lose interest any skills they actually have will deteriorate further.

Record-keeping is indispensable in order to know whether dogs are guessing, or seeing cues. A record must be kept of every instance when the dog alerts and whether drugs were found. That is the only way to know the dog's error rate (how often the dog provides false positives) or to discover whether the dog is merely used for official lies. Only with record keeping and independent testing can any judge draw any conclusion from the dog's "game playing" out on the street.

Any criminal case with inadequate record-keeping about a dog should result in suppression of the evidence and dismissal of the charges against the defendant.

Dogs approximate humans in that they go along with the system to avoid disapproval from peers. Humans crave approval from supervising officers, other police, teachers, classmates, friends, et cetera. Drug dogs crave approval from their police handlers. Dogs play the game, and will try to guess and read cues (subconscious cues or deliberate cues), because the dogs are searching for approval, not for drugs.

Dogs mimic humans in that they can be trained (brainwashed) to do hurtful things – such as passing the 18th amendment (the old prohibition) in the case of humans. In the dogged pursuit of modern prohibition, some dogs are slow learners, as are some humans.

The government's war on drugs is a dog chasing its own tail.

Let's liberate drug dogs. Return them to protecting people from violence and theft, which is also the only proper purpose of law enforcement. Dogs should be man's best friend, not man's persecutor.

# 4

# COURT CASE:
# ILLINOIS V. CABALLES

Drug dog fraud was encouraged in January 2005, under the U.S. Supreme Court case of *Illinois vs. Caballes* (not one of Dr. Curry's cases), holding that a dog sniff during a traffic stop was not a "search." Caballes involved a allegedly "legitimate" traffic stop for speeding (that turned into 12 years in prison for marijuana).

*Caballes* is interpreted to mean that cops can take dogs fishing. *Caballes* and similar cases turn canines into props for lies. When dogs are used as props for lies, it doesn't matter whether dogs are well-trained.

The *Caballes* case from the U.S. Supreme Court foreshadows more police-state possibilities: Uniformed law enforcement marching through neighborhoods with German shepherds on leashes sniffing anything and everything -every car parked on or near the street, the air emanating from homes, neighbors walking outside.

Imagine the same thing at any place of business or employment, and police marching German shepherds through parking lots, car to car, for no reason other than fishing expeditions. Imagine the same nightmare in any shopping area or a downtown street area, a festival, a bar's parking lot. Uniformed agents with German shepherds sniffing pedestrians and their bags and cars and anything. The uniformed harassing the uninformed searching purses, pockets, cars, et cetera, on the streets.

Police-state tactics were witnessed worldwide via videotape from Stratford High School in Goose Creek, South Carolina, where police used dogs in a surprise "raid" for students inside of a school.

No drugs were found in the raid of the Goose Creek school.

In other schools, classes have been interrupted and the children were marched out and lined up to be harassed by a dog.

What next? Cops with barking German Shepherds marching through classrooms every morning to sniff each child during the robotic chanting of the Pledge of Allegiance in the police-state camps known as government schools. If so, that would give the government another excuse to re-impose the Pledge of Allegiance's earlier Nazi salute. That will be another way in which the U.S. police state resembles the National Socialist German Workers Party (Nazis).

The police state in the U.S. is nothing new. Francis Bellamy (author of the Pledge of Allegiance, and the origin of the Nazi salute and Nazi behavior) wrote the pledge to promote the government's takeover of schools. Bellamy was a self-proclaimed socialist and touted (along with his cousin Edward Bellamy) what he called "military socialism."

The Bellamy cousins wanted government to use socialized schools to achieve their goals. They inspired trite propaganda in which every "problem" spirals into a war: the War on Drugs, the War on Poverty, the War on Crime, the War on Illiteracy, the War on Terrorism, et cetera. They inspired the use of government force and violence for any and all purposes. Today, the U.S.'s military-socialist complex and its aggressive military socialism is the Bellamy dogma.

The government's schools will not teach children about their Constitutional rights, including their 4th Amendment rights against searches (including the right to refuse to consent to searches, to say "NO!" to searches), and their right to remain silent (to refuse to answer questions when a police officer barks at them).

The Pledge of Allegiance is obedience training for humans: stand, speak, sit, roll over, attack, play dead.....

Guardians of groupthink believe that any American who "loves freedom" must chant robotically, salute and sing whenever someone barks a command to do so.

# 5

# LAWYERS & NARCOTICS DOGS

In an article entitled "Free the Drug Dogs!" at the History News Network (of George Mason University) the writer Keith Halderman stated, *"... attorney Rex Curry, who was one of the first libertarians I ever met, and who helped transform much of my thinking, developed a case that may be headed to the Supreme Court. [The case], which he won, involves a challenge to the veracity of drug dogs searches. The state of Florida is appealing and the issue is on the high court's docket."*

A professional dog trainer wrote about Dr. Curry: *"... you did our profession a great favor. Maybe we can get rid of the B.S. trainers and the monkey-see-monkey-do method to training, and apply the science behind it."*

DrugSense Weekly journal published an interview asking, *"Given the problems with drug dogs explored in your work, why do you think they are so popular with police departments and municipal government?"*

Dr. Curry's answer was, *"Oh that is easy. You have to remember that there is a strong incentive for law enforcement not to CARE whether the dogs are accurate. The dogs can simply be props for lies, in that the dogs are there to overcome refusals to consent to search, and the dog provides law enforcement officers (LEOs) with the ability to say that an alert occurred even if there was no alert. And here is another angle: some LEOs do not want a 'drug dog,' they want a 'car dog,' in that they want a dog that when shown a car will alert, as if to say 'yes that is a car.' For some LEOs the goal is to search whenever the LEO desires, period. The dog is simply a ruse to do so. That is why the dogs are so popular. Do not be confused with the idea that there are 'problems with drug dogs.' For some LEOs those are not problems at all. And again, that is why some LEOs have no interest in maintaining records about their dogs."*

Many people write with responses to the ongoing research about drug dogs, including this one: *"I discovered a vacant lot where some dog-cops were meeting and I saw them signal training the dogs to 'GO OFF' on cue with very slight hand motions. Then I saw them walk dogs around a COP car they used (this shows it will work in any situation) and when the cop made this*

*little twitch with one finger extended, the dog would bite
at the door handle and tires and stand on its back legs
and bark at the windows etc..."*

The Libertarian Lawyer was interviewed about drug
dogs in Playboy magazine, and that prompted another
drug dog expert to quip: *"Dr. Curry made it in to
Playboy Magazine without taking his clothes off."*

The police state (and the use of drug dogs) is
becoming an international problem, as evidenced by this
excerpt of a communication from abroad:

*"I wonder if I could please ask for some help? We are
a children's civil rights organisation based in the UK. As
you are probably aware, there has been a rise in the use
of drugs sniffer dogs here. In some schools, dogs are
taken in to perform routine searches, and it is now
commonplace in London to have dogs posted at the exits
to London underground trains.*

*While we have been concerned about the use of dogs,
and had objected on various civil liberties grounds, we
had naively assumed that dogs were pretty accurate!
We've found out the hard way that this isn't true: two of
our (non-drug-using) teenaged members have now been
stopped by dogs at stations, and then searched. They
were both pretty upset by the experience.*

*We want to find all the research possible about the
accuracy of sniffer dogs, and intend to bring out a report*

*to publicise what is going on. – quite honestly, we are more likely to stop the practice of going into schools with dogs in this way, rather than by arguing civil liberties (not a major concern of the British public!)*

[from "Action on Rights for Children"]

The description of the police-state in the U.K. (from the comments above) are similar to the U.S.'s police state. People in Britain and worldwide witnessed police-state tactics in the U.S. via videotape from Stratford High School in Goose Creek, South Carolina, where police used dogs in a surprise "raid" for students inside of a school. Those images are available in any web search.

Similar behavior may be in store for the UK if it has not already happened there.

A lawyer revealed: *"A judge in my local county was stopped for speeding and was treated like dirt by the cop. That's one judge who woke up."*

Government's attitude toward your liberty is like a dog at a fire hydrant. The difference is that the government will pee on your head and tell you that it is raining.

Don't "Howl Hitler" – instead, stop the U.S.'s police state.

# ABOUT THE AUTHOR

Before becoming a full-time writer, Ian Tinny was a part-time instructor to the United States Probation Office and to federal judges, and his work led to the arrest, trial, conviction, and imprisonment of America's Dumbest Criminals.

In addition to the above, Tinny was a personal effectiveness coach specializing in cognitive and behavior change development for individuals and teams, and he was an animal behaviorist.

Tinny is also the author of the groundbreaking book "Pledge of Allegiance + Swastika Secrets" available at http://www.amazon.com/dp/148121618X   It is a semi-biographical work about the nation's leading authority on the Pledge of Allegiance, who exposed (1) the pledge as the origin of the Nazi salute and Nazi behavior, and (2) how German socialists (Nazis) used the swastika to represent crossed "S" letters for "socialism."

Tinny collects old photos and film footage of the early Pledge of Allegiance showing the origin of the notorious stiff-armed salute.

Tinny is also the author of a classic science fiction tale revealing an amazing discovery about time travel. http://www.amazon.com/dp/1500588091

Tinny operates Ian Tinny Literary Productions and Consulting. He resides in Key West, Florida, for most of the year, with his dog (pictured on the cover) and his cat, overlooking the water. When not in Key West, he spends time in Manhattan.